OYA

SANTERIA AND THE ORISHA OF STORMS

By Baba Raul Canizares

ORIGINAL PUBLICATIONS
Visit us on the WEB:
www.OCCULT1.com
Telephone: 1 (888) OCCULT-1

OYA
SANTERIA AND THE ORISHA OF THE WINDS
© 2006 by Original Publications

ISBN: 0-942272-87-0

All rights reserved. No part of this book may be reproduced in any manner whatsoever, including Internet usage, without written permission from Original Publications, except in the case of brief quotations embodied in critical reviews and articles.

The author and publisher offer this book for interest, folkloric value, experimentation and whatever value it may have to the reader. Please be advised that we cannot make any claim of supernatural effects or powers for any of the methods or interpretations made herein. The book is offered as literary curio only. No responsibility whatsoever for the contents or veracity of the statements herein is assumed by the author or publisher or seller of this book.

FIRST EDITION

First Printing 2006

Cover Art and Illustrations
by Baba Raul Canizares
Frontispiece and Back Cover Art
by Eric K. Lerner

INTRODUCTION

Here comes Iansa

With her luminous crown!

Here comes Iansa

With the wind and rain.

She travels the forest,

Flying over hills.

Here comes Iansa,

Queen of the wind and rain.[1]

Long before the women's liberation movement flowered in America, African women had an inspiring role model in Oya, queen of the Nupe., warrior wife of the great king of the Yoruba, Shango. Strong as an ox and more potent than lightning, Oya rules over storms, witchcraft, markets, the Niger river, and spirit mediums—called egungun. She is also associated with the rainbow, for she is said to wear a gown of many colors (wini wini). Oya rules the Nupe nation as an independent queen (oba). Her position as wife of Shango made her queen-consort of the Yoruba as well. Even though she married the most powerful king of the region, she did not surrender her independent stature as a monarch in her own right.

In Cuban Santeria Oya is the ruler of the lightning bolt, indefatigable warrior queen who accompanies Shango in all of his campaigns. He is the thunder whose rumble sends fear to the hearts of men, but she is he electrical discharge that actually kills them. Oya is also the whistling sound of the wind and the patron orisha of death, in this garb she is visualized by Cubans as the one who guards the gates of cemetery and by Africans as the orisha who protects the egungun society, the Yoruba masqueraders/mediums who possess the power to channel ancestral spirits. Oya is also called Yansan, "Mother of nine," alluding to her four sets of twins and her son Abiku, "he who is born to die." The name Oya itself means "the tearer," alluding to her destructive force. She is similar to the Hindu goddess Kali and the Greek Hecate, and represents the archetype of the destructive Mother who performs the necessary destruction which allows for regeneration and growth.

Along with Shango, Oshun, Obatala, Eleggua, Yemaya, and Ogun, Oya is one of Santeria's Seven African Powers, the seven most frequently invoked deities in the Lukumi[2] pantheon and the most frequently "seated" in a person's consciousness ("seating" refers to the act of initiating a priest or priestess). The Spanish word "potencias, " rendered as "powers," is really not accurately translated in the present context. A more accurate rendering would be "empowering," for these seven deities are by and large the ones that empower practitioners to triumph in life. As an agent of empowerment, especially for women, Oya has no equal.

1
Sacred Stories About Oya

Oya, Ogun, and Shango
And How Ogun Invented Farm Tools

According to an ancient story, Oya , the elegant warrior-queen of the Nupe nation, entered into an arranged marriage with the Yoruba demigod Ogun, Lord of the Forge[3], inventor of iron weapons. Ogun's uncouth ways, however, eventually got on Oya's nerves, for although Oya was the equal of any man in a field of battle, she was a refined lady when not fighting. Ogun, on the other hand, was a consummate man of the army, more comfortable in all-male barracks than in the company of a refined woman. When the extraordinarily beautiful orisha of thunder, Shango, came around intent on seducing Oya, she didn't put on much of a fight. In the fiery king of Oyo, Oya found her soulmate.

An African myth states that when Oya left Ogun she took the seven iron weapons he had invented with her. It was at this point that Ogun decided to create something different out of iron, inventing seven tools used for farming and agriculture. This sacred tale records the transition of men from warrior nomads to settled agriculturists, from transient cave-dwellers to builders of cities, from ancient hunter gatherers to modern urbanites.

The story of how Oya left Ogun to become Shango's mate goes as follows. The day he decided to seduce Oya he had his long, reddish hair oiled and braided, he then rubbed his sister Oshun's potent love honey all over his body, and borrowed his father's crimson cape and white crown made of cowry shells. Mounted on his magnificent white stallion Eshinla, Shango presented such a vision that several humans who looked at him were overwhelmed by such beauty, losing their reason. Others committed suicide, knowing they would never see anything so beautiful again. Arriving at Ogun's hut, Shango was astounded to see a woman who so looked like him that for a moment he thought his brother Eshu was playing one of his shape-shifting pranks.

"Oya?" asked Shango sheepishly.

"That's right, and judging by your conceited appearance you must be Shango."

This was not what Shango had planned. The beautiful woman standing in front of his horse was actually looking at him with insolence, with disdain almost!

Trying to retain his composure, Shango declared in his most theatrical tone: "I've come to take you with me."

"Ha!' Said Oya, "What makes you think I'd want to go with you?"

Santeria and the Orisha of the Winds — 5

"Why, I'm the most beautiful man in the universe!"

"Really? Well, let me tell you something, boy, with the lights out and under the covers, all men are the same. It's what happens outside the sleeping mat that really counts."

At that point Shango realized that he had fallen madly in love with this insolent queen.

"Look, I know Ogun works day and night, so he has no time to satisfy a fiery woman like you, come with me and I'll make love to you in ways you never dreamed of."

"Would you fight for me?"

"I'll tear Ogun apart for you."

"It's not Ogun I want you to fight, boy" said Oya while reaching under her voluminous skirts. Taking out two huge swords, one in each hand, she began to twirl like a tornado, sending lightning all around, knocking Shango off his horse and beating him senseless with her swords. When he came to, he was totally confused.

"Don't feel bad" a smiling Oya told the badly battered youth "I used the element of surprise to my great advantage."

"I was never defeated before, and I've fought every warrior except Ogun."

"Ogun doesn't let me go to battle, yet I was born a warrior. Tell you what, if you let me stand with you in your battles, I'll go with you. How do you feel about women fighting like men?"

"Why, I don't mind, ask my sister Dada, she is my most trusted fighting partner!"

"Then lets go, boy, we have a long way ahead of us." Jumping behind Shango, Oya hugged his slender waist, gently resting her head on his broad back as Eshinla rode towards Orishaland.

Word reached Ogun that his beautiful wife had deserted him for Shango. Enraged, he swore to kill his brother and get his wife back. Reaching the outskirts of Orishaland, Ogun was met by Eshu, who told him he could not ever enter there because of something that had transpired many years before between him and his mother. Reluctantly, Ogun went back to his house, swearing to someday avenge his loss.

The Mother of Nine

Some Afro-Cuban traditions name Oya as the mother of the twin gods called Ibeji. Others name Oshun. In reality, most Yoruba goddesses are thought to have given birth to twins. Oya's praise name, Yansa (Mother of nine), is said to recall that she is the mother of four sets of twins and a boy named Abiku. In my lineage it is said that Shango and Oya are the parents of the Ibeji, while Abiku is Ogun and Oya's child. The story of how Oya came to have nine children is told in the Odu Ifa (chapter of the holy book of Ifa) Osa Meji. According to that odu, Oya suffered from constant miscarriages until she consulted a babalawo, who told her to bring money to Orunla, as well as an ewe and a cloth of many colors. She did as she was told, which included her eating of the meat of the ewe. After that she had four sets of twins and a son named "Egungun" (or, depending on the source, "Abiku"). Since that time, Oya does not eat ewe, and neither do her followers. Osa meji mentions Oya's ties to the all-important society of the Egungun, whose role it is to channel the spirits of the dead, an enormously important function in a world that is centered on offering veneration to the ancestors. Osa Meji also describes Oya as protector of women who sell in the marketplace. Another Odu Ifa that talks about Oya is Osa Ogunda, which tells the story of how Ogun made her marry him when he found out she could transform herself into a buffalo (efon).

Oya and Shango

Why Royal Palm Trees Attract Lightning

Although in everyday speech Shango is called the Orisha of Lightning, elders in Santeria have always maintained that dominion over electrical discharges belongs to Shango's fiery wife Oya. One of Lydia Cabrera's elderly informants, speaking in the early 1940's, relates how Shango, an irrepressible womanizer, would climb on top of a royal palm tree that grew in back of Oya's palace in order to "check out the beauties behind Oya's back, exchanging hand signals with them."[4] Oya became suspicious of her royal mate's increased passion for palm tree climbing, so she began to spy on him. When Shango wasn't present, she would climb the royal palm to see what could be seen from there. Luckily for Shango, Oya did not perceive anything unusual on her first try, but promised herself she would go up that palm tree at different hours, until she found out what was going on. Shango, however, became aware that Oya had climbed the palm without telling him. Knowing his wife's dislike for lizards, Shango, who rules over them, arranged to have hundreds of the little creatures hide in the tree, telling them to come out whenever Oya would attempt to climb the palm again. As soon as Oya started her climb up the thin, long trunk, hundreds of lizards began to fall on her like raindrops. Using her God-given power over lightning, Oya immediately struck the palm tree. Whenever a lightning bolt hits a royal palm tree, the elders say that Oya is letting out her anger at Shango's servile little lizards.

Commentary: More than a morality lesson, this pataki appears to be one of a number of sacred stories designed to explain all natural events using the archetypal imagery associated with Orisha. Rather than believing the tale literally, most elders would point out at how Oya's ownership of lightning is emphasized, as well as her right to act and think independently. Many Afro-Cuban pataki show women playing remarkably strong roles, an especially astounding fact when one considers the status of women in Latin American society.

Santeria and the Orisha of the Winds

Oya, the Raging Storm

Oya Frees Shango From Prison

Although traditionally three goddesses were associated with Shango as his consorts: Oba, Oshun, and Oya, it is Oya that is his true soulmate, his shakti, the yin to his yang. In Cuban Santeria, Oya is often described as fighting by the side of her king, two sabres ablazing, creating lightning as she rides into battle to win the war with her man. An often-told pataki relates how Shango once became so drunk while traveling incognito through a land not his own that he was placed under arrest in that land's king's castle. Upon realizing who their distinguished prisoner was, the king ordered seven enchanted chains to be tied around Shango so that he couldn't escape. The king debated if he should ask for ransom or just take over Shango's vast empire. Becoming concerned about her beloved Shango's whereabouts, Oya went over to his magic pestle, where Shango usually saw as in a vision all he wanted to see. Using Shango's divining pestle with expertise, Oya saw her husband enveloped in chains. Horrified, Oya chanted the following magic formula: "Centella que va bene Yo sumarela sube Centella que va bene Yo sube arriba palo."

Not an instant passed when Oya said this and a giant number " 7" appeared in the heavens, turning into a lightning bolt that descended to where Shango was chained, hitting the chains and making them fall away from Shango. Once freed from the chains, the Lord of Thunder easily escaped his captors. On that day, Shango learned just how powerful his queen consort was. His respect for Oya's strength grew as he realized that not only was she his soul mate, but his equal in strength.

Commentary: Pataki pointing out Oya's physical prowess are many. Her stories serve as constant reminders to women that they can do whatever a man can do. Daughters of Oya serve as role models for womankind, demonstrating that a woman's place is not necessarily in the home, but wherever she wishes it to be. As able ruler, consummate warrior, devoted spouse and fiery lover, Oya is the epitome of a fully realized woman.

Oya Uses Iku to Keep Shango Captive

One of Oya's best friends was the only being Shango feared, Iku, the embodiment of death. Shango, vital, life itself, could not stand the presence of the lord of the dead. Whenever Iku would visit Oya, she would warn Shango ahead of time so he could be as far away from her palace as possible. Feeling neglected by Shango, thinking he was spending more time with his other wives than with her, Oya devised a plan to keep Shango with her. She told Iku to stay right outside her palace while Shango was inside. His fear of death was such that he would not leave as long as Iku was there.

"Oya, tell that accursed thing to get the hell out so I can go my way," an irate Shango ordered.

Feigning innocence, Oya pleaded "But Shango, Iku does not listen to me anymore. What can I do to force him?"

And so it was that days turned into weeks and weeks into months as everyone wondered where their king was. Because he had instituted strong councils to rule in his absence, the government of Oyo was never threatened, but people began to wonder what was going on. Seeing what was happening, Eshu went to visit his brother.

"Oh, Eshu, I am I glad to see You!" Exclaimed an exasperated Shango, "Tell this accursed ajogun [demon] to get out."

"I can't do that, Shango, for Oya was owed a favor from Iku and she has chosen to ask for this, which I cannot transgress…There is one way, however, you might get out"

"What? I'll do anything!"

Capitalizing on Shango's remarkable resemblance to Oya, Eshu dressed him up to look just like her. Imitating Oya's voice, the dressed-up Shango told Iku to leave, which he did thinking it was Oya who had told him. When Oya came home, she found Shango had escaped. She feared what he would do to her. When later that week Oya met with her husband and he acted as if nothing had happened, a not-too-small smile of triumph spread over Oya's face.

Commentary: In this pataki Oya uses unusual methods to achieve her goal, which is to force her husband to spend more time with her at home. Although her actions may seem extreme, the goddess is simply giving voice to all those women who are constantly neglected by their husbands, who leave them alone in the household as virtual domestic prisoners while they go to and fro without a care in the world.

Oya Helps Shango Defeat Ogun In battle

Ogun's feud with Shango, which had started when Shango stole Oya away from Ogun, had escalated to all-out war. Ogun actually raised an army to meet Shango's army in battle. Ogun's domain over warfare and his familiarity with the dense jungle made him practically indestructible in the depths of the bush. When Shango decided to take his army into the jungle to battle Ogun, all of his advisors told him he wouldn't be able to defeat the Lord of Iron in his domain. Stubborn and proud, Shango ignored all advice and headed with all his forces towards the jungle, telling Oya not to go with him this time because she had been married to Ogun before. As predicted, Shango's army was soon decimated by the forces of Ogun, since Ogun's forces were protected by Osanyin, Lord of all Vegetation, and trained by Oshosi, Lord of the Hunt. Just when it seemed as if Shango would have to concede defeat, Oya, who had surreptitiously followed Shango to battle, began to shake her nine skirts vigorously, sending storms of such magnitude to the forces of Ogun that every soldier, every tree, every stone, in fact, every thing in sight was either killed, uprooted, or pushed back one hundred miles. A large desert appeared where jungles had thrived. In order to save what little forest remained, Ogun admitted defeat.

Commentary: When Shango ordered Oya to stay behind as he went to fight her ex-husband, Ogun, Oya did not listen to him; she disobeyed

Santeria and the Orisha of the Winds — 13

Oya, the Warrior Queen

her husband, following him into battle. By doing this, she won the battle for him. This pataki posits Oya as an original thinker strong enough to assess that by disobeying her husband she would actually be doing him a greater service than if she blindly obeyed him.

The Moving Story Of Moremi

A profoundly moving, semi-historical pataki passed down in my family in Cuba but obviously originating in the city-state of Oyo, in Africa, has to do with an avatar of Oya named Moremi. As the story goes, Obara, king of the Yoruba, had decided to marry a very young girl from the neighboring kingdom of Nupe said to bear all nine markings identifying her as the goddess Oya. Obara fell in love with the girl when she was fourteen and he had spied her bathing in the River Niger. Moremi's father was a humble farmer, she therefore did not qualify to be a royal wife, her supposed divine status not withstanding. Her parents considered it an honor to have their young daughter join the royal household as a concubine. Obara so loved Moremi, however, that he flaunted custom firstly by elevating Moremi to the status of royal wife on her sixteenth birthday, then naming her yalode or primary consort on her eighteenth birthday. In fact, the truth was that Obara was in a state of virtual monogamy with his lovely young queen. At a time of war, when a band of seemingly extra-terrestrial beings was taking over Oyo, the king's divining priests prophesied that the unassuming Moremi would lead the country to victory over the terrifying demons that were taking over Oyo.

Moremi offered Eshu a goat, asking him for guidance. Eshu told Moremi to go to a lagoon where Olokun, terrifying divinity of the ocean, was locally worshipped. There she would find her answer. Going to the lagoon, Moremi was kidnapped by the horrifying demons. Moremi was originally from Nupe, so she understood the Nupe dialect. She was therefore surprised to hear the demons speaking in Nupe!

They were talking among themselves about how superstitious and gullible the Oyo people were, how they let their—the supposed demons's disguises, made up of raffia and palm fronds, fool them into thinking they were supernatural beings, how the Oyo were practically giving their hard-earned empire away to the disguised Nupe out of irrational fear! Arriving at the royal castle of Nupeland, the "demons" took off their disguises and presented the young queen to their king, Oba Tapa. Oba Tapa fell immediately in love with Moremi and ordered her to be prepared for marriage. Moremi pretended to go along, but she escaped a few days later, returning to Oyo with the news that the attackers were not demons, just disguised men from Nupe. With this information in hand, the Oyo warriors were able to defeat their attackers, not only forcing them to retreat, but actually making Nupe a vassal state of Oyo. The sad part of the story is that upon going back to the lagoon to ask Olokun what he wanted for his having helped Oyo, the terrifying orisha demanded to have Moremi's first child. Much to Obara's regret, Moremi convinced him that he must allow her to honor Olokun's request. One year later Moremi bore a son which she gave to Olokun. For her great sacrifice Moremi is still honored in Oyo with a yearly observance marking the anniversary of her sacrifice, where everyone sings her praises with the words "For her country, she gave her child." It is said that Moremi never fully recovered from the loss of her first born, so when some years later she bore another boy for the king, she gave the baby to his father and then she cried herself into the waters of the River Niger, which became indistinguishable from herself! In this manner Moremi became an active deity, the fluid form of Oya, with her waters nurturing the whole Niger valley.

The remarkable African-American priestess of Oshun and author Luisah Teish recounts the following pataki in her elegant work *Jambalaya* (San Francisco:: Harper Collins, 1985):

Whirling Wind was the one who cast Ifa for Nine Skirts on the day she hear the cry, "Help, Oya, help me to change." The human held no pain and said, "My head is dizzy with ugly thoughts, my belly is hard with greed, my knees are weak with the weight of guilt, and the leaves will not cure me." Oya spun around on her toes. The human cried, "What must I do for you, Oya, what is your price for my cure?" Oya spun around on her fingers. "Must I give you all my gold? Must I surrender my ego? Shall I beg your forgiveness?" Oya spun around on her head. The human screamed and cried, "Please, Twirling Woman, Help me. Help me!" Oya flashed her dark mirror and said, "If you wish release, human, simply look into my mirror and change. You who need courage, look into my mirror and change. If you desire wisdom, simply look into my mirror and change. Power can be yours if you will look into my mirror and change." And so the human looked into her mirror and changed! "Oh, Oya, my head is clear, my belly soft, my knees are strong. What must I do to pay you for this wonder?" Oya took a wide-legged step and she fanned her skirts just so. And all the curing leaves fell from the trees and laid a path before the human. Whirling wind was the one who cast Ifa for Nine Skirts on the day she heard the cry. Oya smiled and said, "You who seek transformation need only look into my mirror . . . and change!"[5]

2
ATTRIBUTES

Necklace: Oya's necklaces vary. One made up of dark brown or brownish-red beads is popular, as is one made of beads that are brownish-red striped with white, or striped with white and black. A brown necklace featuring clusters of nine different color beads interspersed throughout is also popular.

Shrine (igbodu) How initiates honor Oya: Oya's secrets are usually kept in a covered china or porcelain pot painted in nine colors, or a dark brown or red one. These "secrets" or "mysteries" include the following: Nine river stones, nine miniature copper tools, such as a shovel, a pick, a hoe, and so forth. Also, a crown from which nine nails hang. Nine copper bracelets are also part of Oya's "herramientas" (tools). Oya is a queen, so her shrine can be adorned with a black iruke, the horse-tail scepter sported by Yoruba royalty. Oya is usually greeted with the salutation "Hekua, Yansa!"

Shrine (olujo alejo) How non-initiates may begin to honor Oya: An altar containing a photograph of lightning, tornadoes, or hurricanes can be set up by those wishing to honor Oya. Plaster skulls, an image of St. Therese of the Child Jesus, or a representation of a rainbow can also serve as points of focus for Oya.

Offerings (adimu): Oya's favorite offering is an eggplant. Fritters made of ground black-eyed peas and white, steamed rice are also suitable as offerings to Oya. She also favors red wine, chocolate pudding, black grapes, figs and star apples.

Blood offerings (ebo): Black hens, guinea fowl, female goat, brown pigeons. Her taboos are ram and turtle. Her ritual foods may not be prepared in pots that have held either of these.

Characteristics of Oya (and of her children): Oya is a riverine goddess, just like Oshun and Oba. She rules over the river Niger. She also rules over marketplaces and the gates of cemeteries. Oya protects against lightning, electrocution, hurricanes, storms, and lung diseases. Oya's devotees tend to be strong, willful, authoritarian women. Children of Oya may be prone to violence, jealousy, and infidelity; yet they are also extremely loyal, sensual, and strong.

Herbs and plants: Purple avocado, plum, eggplant, witch hazel, vervain, papaya, royal poinciana, camphor, tamarind, poppy, altamisa, wild cucumber.

Roads of Oya: Yansa Oriri; Oya Obini Nupe; Oya Mimu; Oya de Koso; Oya Yeku Yeku.

In Arara religion Oya is called Dale, in Palo she is known as Centella Ndoki, Remolino, and Mariwanga. In Vodou she is Aizan. Oya's Catholic disguises in Cuba include St. Therese of the Child Jesus and Our Lady of Candlemas.

Oya in Brazil: In Brazil, she is called Oia and Iansa by the Nagos, Sobo by the Jejes, Matamba by the Angolas, Nunvurucomabuva by the Congos, and Bamburucemas by the Bantu. She is syncretized with St. Barbara. She receives offerings of hens and she-goats, but hates rams. Brazilians salute Oya with the praise "epa-hei!" Her colors in

Santeria and the Orisha of the Winds

Oya's devotees may be stong, unconventional, domineering women.

Brazil are red and white, her necklace is dark red. She is symbolized by her sabre, her royal horse tail scepter (iruke in Lukumi, Eruexim in Brazilian Nago), and a buffalo horn.

In Umbanda (Afro-Brazilian spiritism) she is called Inhanga, and she is thought to lead the principal legions of spirits under her husband, Xango.

Initiation names: At a recent initiation ceremony, where an Orisha name is selected for the neophyte through the use of the oracle, I was appalled to see that after about seven tries, each time the oracle saying "no" to the name the oriate proposed, the oriate looked blankly around, for he had run out of names! Luckily, those of us who were present and knew other proper names to offer saved the situation. Respected elder Andres Hing (Chango Yemi) published the following list of allowed names for Oya in 1971.

> Oya leti; Oya tokun; Oya tosi; Oya yimi; Oya diosyimi; Oya aina; Oya kule; Oya funke; Oya miwa; Oya dei; Oya kunsho; Oya dina Oya garde; Oya bi; Oya funko; Oya yansa; Oya dumidu; Oya fumito; Oya funshe; Oyalesi; Oyalete; Oya mini; Oya oromu; Oya nina; Oya nike; Oya teki; Oya tilewa; Oya yimii; Oya mimu; Oya obinidodo; Oya ayawa; Oya odo-oya; Yansa oriri.

3
OYA AND SANTERIA'S "CELESTIAL COURT"

Santeria's Mount Olympus is Ile-Ife, where a Zeus-like Obatala presides over a pantheon of gods and heroes. Oya occupies a special niche in this celestial court as the female epitome of transcendental valor. Oya may be a woman, but she has cojones!

Although linked with the troubled and hard-working Ogun in the beginning of her story, it is as Shango's fiery consort that Oya truly shines. Her incredible exploits as a superb warrior and her frequent good-natured war of wills with Shango present Oya as a different kind of woman, a non-traditionalist, an iconoclast, a feminist. Along with the other two wives of Shango, the super-domestic Oba and the sensuous Oshun, Oya presents women with a variety of choices.

It is said that if Oya is wrongly installed in a person's consciousness, death will be the result, not just for the iyawo, but for the initiator as well. Because of her uniqueness, Oya tends to be somewhat frightening. In Cuban Santeria she is widely respected, but does not enjoy the kind of mass appeal Oshun and Shango have. When a neophyte undergoes a reading to find out who his or her head orisha is, he or she may be somewhat startled when told it is Oya. Later on, however, the child of Oya will learn to love the powerful orisha whose passions are as sweeping as the tornadoes she rules.

Oya, queen of the Nupe, queen consort of Oyo, ruler of the wind, Owner of the Marketplace, and the River Niger personified, fills a unique niche in Santeria's celestial court. She shows women how to live life fully and independently. In this way she also shows women that, just as she is with Shango because she wants to, not because she has to, they too can enjoy relationships with men based on mutual respect and unconditional love, not on a need for shelter and protection. Oya presents a modern paradigm women in the 21st century can identify with.

4

ORIKI OYA & ORIN OYA

PRAYERS & SONGS TO OYA

Those who have been initiated as priests and priestesses in Santeria can increase the power of cleansings and works they do with Oya by reciting praise verses called "oriki" and by singing praise songs called "Orin" (also called "suyere") to the Orisha. Following are some oriki and Orin in Lukumi that have been in use in Cuba for hundreds of years. Speakers of standard Yoruba should be able in most cases to recognize the meaning of the Lukumi words.

Oriki

Obirin t' o t' ori

ogun da 'rungbon si

Efufulele ti

'da 'gi l'oke-1'-oke

A-su-'jo ma ro

In the field of war you fight as a bearded man

You are the mighty wind that tears down trees from top to bottom

You can make an ominous dark cloud yet withhold the rain

Oriki

Ogun da 'rungbon si, Iyalode

Orisa me-'n-di-1'-ogun

ni mbe 1' odo Sango,

ni'bi k's san'pa, ni'bi k'a yan,

1'Oya fi gb'oko I' owo won.

You are tall and bearded, yet no woman is comelier than you, my queen.

Your gaze is so potent none dare behold it, your wrath so devastating it must be avoided

Of all sixteen maiden goddesses, Shango chose to marry you

Because of your grace and elegance of movement.

Orin

Bembe Oya,

Oya la finda E-ee,

Oya la finda,

Santa Teresa,

Oya la finda E-ee.

The tearer thrives Like the ruler of a great forest, like St. Therese, Tearer rules the great forest.

Orin

(This mostly Spanish song from Oriente province, Cuba, reflects that area's non-traditional approach to orisha worship)

Hoy hay toque de bembe

En el cabildo de Oya

En la fiesta que le brindan

Los hijos de Obatala

Iyankamae Iyankama-o

Si to me abres las puertas

yo to dara de comer.

Today a feast is going on

In the temple of Oya

It is a feast being offered

by the sons of Obatala

Oh great Mother of the Dead,

Oh great ruler of death,

Clear my paths,

accept my sacrifice

Orin

Eremi ose Oya,

Opakarakoloro,

Kalakalawo,

onikaralawo o le le,

O wimi o wimi,

O le le.

Oya mensameji,

O le le,

Oya mensaemu,

O le le

You provide me with profit, Oya. Your loudness is sign of your wealth.

Look at the many hues, the wealth of our loud queen, strong and responsible.

She is so strong! She is so strong! Strong and responsible

She makes it rain eighteen times as much, She is strong and responsible.

She makes nine rains do her cleaning, She is strong and responsible.

5
DESPOJOS

CLEANSINGS & SPELLS WITH OYA

Oya is a great queen and as such she demands fine foods. She especially likes eggplant in any form, boiled, fried, exquisitely prepared or even raw. Preparing a fine meal for Oya, then passing the meal (on a plate) over your body before discarding it in a cemetery is an excellent cleansing to rid yourself of bad vibrations and bring the blessing of good fortune to your household.

Oya's favorite dish is called frituras de caritas, this is how we prepare it in my house: Take a cup of boiled black-eyes peas. Grind in a food processor along with an egg. Heat 1/4 cup of oil on a frying pan until moderately hot, drop spoonfuls of the mixture into hot oil, brown on both sides, drain in paper towel. Add salt only if people will partake.

It is said that Oya will grant you any wish if you give her nine small eggplants. The way to do this is to present them to the goddess on a large plate along with a red ribbon and a lighted seven-day brown or dark red candle. After nine days, pack everything including plate and remnants of the candle and throw over a fence of a cemetery at night (preferably at nine).

The most powerful cleansing you can do with Oya is to go to the cemetery, pick up nine stones from nine different graves, leaving nine pennies at each site where you have picked a stone. Take all nine stones to your home and pray to Oya each night over a lighted candle while watching the stones, asking for what you want removed from your life. On the ninth night, gather all the stones and return them to the cemetery. Your petition will be duly granted!

OYA'S LOVE SPELLS

Take a pigeon's heart, oil of cloves, olive oil, almond oil, nine straight pins, witch hazel, red mercury. Write the names of the two people who are to be made to fall in love on a brown paper bag. Mix all ingredients and place inside bag. After nine days throw the bag over fence of cemetery along with nine pennies

Another love spell goes like this. Write the name of the person you want to influence on a piece of parchment. Pierce a guinea hen's heart with nine straight pins. Add a smooth surfaced river stone, red mercury, and rock candy. Place all ingredients on a plate. Light candles to it for nine consecutive days. After nine days, discard inside a cemetery. It will turn an indifferent man or woman into a sensuous, athletic lover.

Another love spell using Oya's powerful energy involves writing the name of the person you want to make your lover on a piece of parchment, using dragon's blood. Then draw the sigill depicted on the next page.

Then anoint parchment with come to me oil, place under a seven-day multi-colored candle., When candle is consumed, bury everything in a desolate corner of a cemetery.

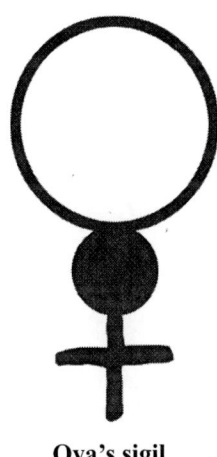

Oya's sigil

OYA'S SEPARATION SPELL

To make a couple split you need two stones you had gathered inside a cemetery (pick each stone as far away from the other as possible), two black seven-day pull-out candles, and a black cord nine and a half feet long. On the night after a full moon place each of the two stones on top of each candle and place candles right next to each other. Name the candles after the people you wish to separate, write each name using a sharp instrument on the side of the candles and anoint with damnation oil. Tie cord around each candle, light them at midnight, separate candles by about one foot, snuff out candles after an hour. The following night, do the same. On the ninth night, the candles should be nine feet away from each other and the cord that unites them should be tight between them. Get a scissors and cut the cord; allow candles to burn out on their own. After candles have been consumed on their own, place each candle with respective stone and piece of cord on two different plastic bags along with four pennies for each bag. Get two different people to deliver each package to a different cemetery, while you go to a third cemetery and, on the tomb of a young girl who died on a year ending in "nine" you deposit one penny saying: "Hekua-Hey Yansa, you separated the bastards!"

MONEY BATH AND FLOOR WASH

Take nine bunches of parsley, nine small eggplants, nine pennies, and nine drops of patchouli oil, put on your bath water, take bath. After you take bath, use water to wash your floors. Leave all physical remnants of work on a crossroads.

LAMP FOR PEACE AND HARMONY

Get a half-gourd (jicara) that's shaped like a medium-sized bowl (you can buy one at your local botanica). Fill with olive oil, clove oil, silver glitter, patchouli oil, cascarilla[6], and a pinch of sugar, light wick and ask Oya to give your home the peace that is like the center of a tornado, but to keep away its violent fringes. Always mention "In the name of Olofi" when doing this work.

PREGNANCY CHARM

: Place nine pennies, heads up, on the seat of a wooden chair, cover with a multi-colored silk handkerchief, make a pregnant woman sit on the covered pennies while she eats a piece of cooked eggplant, pay the woman at least nine dollars for her service. Collect the pennies and the handkerchief, place inside red flannel bag, sew bag shut, anoint with human placenta oil or shampoo. A woman who wants to get pregnant should have the bag with her each time she has sex. I prepared this charm for a 46 year-old book editor who had never been pregnant. Her husband, who had less than one chance in a thousand of procreating, almost divorced his wife thinking she had cheated when the lady in question promptly became pregnant. DNA tests later on proved their beautiful baby boy was indeed his!

MONEY DRAWING WORK

In an empty coffee can, put the following ingredients: dirt collected in front of nine different banks; nine pebbles collected inside a cemetery, near tombs of very rich people if possible; twenty-seven coins from at least seven different countries; a piece of gold; a piece of silver; nine dollar bills; lavender oil, patchouli, and come-to-me oil. Top all of these ingredients with enough wet plaster to fill the can. When the plaster hardens, paint the whole can gold. Hide somewhere in your home where it won't be disturbed. Money will flow in from all directions.

NINE WISHES WORK

Nine wishes work: Light a multi-colored candle to Oya, ask her to give you clarity as you write down nine things you really wish you could have. Although you may be lofty in your dreams, do not be silly; for instance, if you are a 200 pound four foot-three inch woman of fifty, do not ask Oya to help you win the Miss America pageant!

Write down nine different petitions in nine different pieces of paper, get nine little eggplants, roll up each petition and insert it inside each eggplant. Tie a ribbon to each eggplant, make sure no two ribbons are the same color, and none should be black. Braid all nine ribbons together, with the nine eggplants remaining dangling. Go to a river at 9:00 PM, twirl the nine eggplants several times above your head, using the braid as a slingshot, let them go and fall in the water. Say "Hekua Hey Yansa, Make my wishes come true!" A that point release nine pennies into the water, turn around, and do not speak a single word until you get back home.

YEYITA GARCIA'S ULTIMATE EXORCISM

Centenarian iyalocha Yeyita Garcia called this cleansing "the bomb." She would perform it in houses so haunted that no one would live in them, after Yeyita got through with her cleansing, no negative vibration could survive! Yeyita's spiritual descendants jokingly refer to the cleansing as her "twelve-step program," a pun on Yeyita's well-known intolerance for addictions.

1. Give house a thorough cleaning using a bit of muriatic acid in a large pail of water.
2. Burn sage, patchouli, and frankincense in great quantities.
3. Get a branch of China Berry and strike all walls beginning in the back of the house all the way to the front, throw away branch in the middle of a busy avenue.
4. Splash Florida water all over.
5. Splash Holy Water all over.
6. Add 32 live slugs and plenty of ice cubes to a pail of water, wash floors of the house again.
7. Paint the whole house inside with white paint to which six cascarilla balls have been added.
8. Have a misa (Kardecian seance) on the premises before moving in. Use an experienced and reliable spirit medium to conduct the seance. During the misa, send the spirits that had haunted the place away towards the eternal light.
9. Right after the misa, pass a white pigeon over each of the people who participated in the misa. Holding the pigeon's feet, let it flap its wings as you go from room to room asking Oya to make the pigeon a carrier of all negativity. Let the pigeon fly away with its heavy burden.
10. Bring in drummers and do a "toque" for the ancestors.
11. Offer Oya a guinea hen as thanks for her blessings, cook the bird on the premises and ritualistically eat a piece of it.
12. Bring a babalawo to bless the house and seal all that has been done with Orunla's blessing.

One of my god-sisters said that after doing all these things, both ghouls and exorcisers were so darned tired no wonder all poltergeist activity ceased!

END NOTES

[1] Serge Bramly, *Macumba* (San Francisco: City Lights Books, 1994) p. 11.

[2] The Lukumi or Lucumi are the descendants of Yoruba slaves brought to Cuba during colonial times. "Lukumi" is also synonymous with "Santeria," although some writers tend to use the word when referring to a form of the religion that uses less Catholic iconography.

[3] A controversial pataki states that Obatala banned Ogun from Orishaland after he was caught committing incest with his mother.

[4] Lydia Cabrera, El Monte (Miami: Ediciones Universal, 1986) p. 226.

[5] Luisah Teish, Jambalaya (San Fransisco: Harpercollins, 1985) p.134

[6] Cascarilla, made out of dried eggshells, is the Lukumi equivalent of the ritual chalk (pembe) used in Africa. It is inexpensive and can be purchased at any botanica.

[7] Although some writers have sought to link the word "toque" to Yoruba or Congo roots, this is simply a good Spanish word meaning "play," as in instruments. With that wonderful economy of language that is the hallmark of the Lucumi, the word toque can be properly translated as "ritual playing of drums for the ancestors."

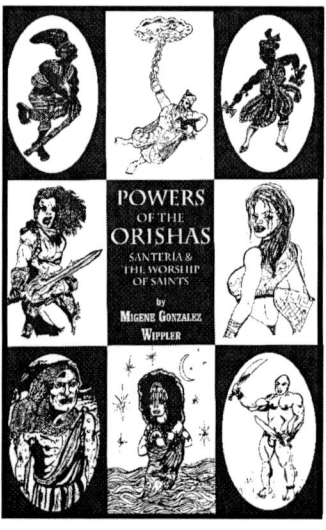

Item #005
$14.95

POWERS OF THE ORISHAS
Santeria and the Worship of Saints
Migene Gonzalez Wippler

Santeria is the Afro-Cuban religion based on an amalgamation between some of the magio-religious beliefs and practices of the Yoruba people and those of the Catholic church. In Cuba where the Yoruba proliferated extensively, they became known as *Lucumi,* a word that means "friendship".

Santeria is known in Cuba as Lucumi Religion. The original Yoruba language, interspersed with Spanish terms and corrupted through the centuries of misuse and mispronunciation, also became known as Lucumi. Today some of the terms used in Santeria would not be recognized as Yoruba in Southwestern Nigeria, the country of origin of the Yoruba people.

Santeria is a Spanish term that means a confluence of saints and their worship. These saints are in reality clever disguises for some of the Yoruba deities, known as Orishas. During the slave trade, the Yoruba who were brought to Cuba were forbidden the practice of their religion by their Spanish masters. In order to continue their magical and religious observances safely the slaves opted for the identification and disguise of the Orishas with some of the Catholic saints worshipped by the Spaniards. In this manner they were able to worship their deities under the very noses of the Spaniards without danger of punishment.

Throughout the centuries the practices of the Yoruba became very popular and soon many other people of the Americas began to practice the new religion.

ISBN 0-942272-25-0 5½"x 8½" 144 pages $9.95

TOLL FREE: 1 (888) OCCULT - 1   **WWW.OCCULT1.COM**

ITEM #001
$16.95

SANTERIA
AFRICAN MAGIC IN LATIN AMERICA

By Migene Gonzalez Wippler

In 1973, the first hardcover edition of *Santeria: African Magic in Latin America* by cultural anthropologist Migene Gonzalez-Wippler was first published by Julian Press. It became an immediate best-seller and is still considered by many experts one of the most popular books on Santeria, having gone through 4 editions and several translations. Now this beloved classic, written by one the foremost scholars on the Afro-Cuban religion, has returned in a 5th edition. This time the text has been carefully edited and corrected to incorporate vital new material. The beliefs, practices, legends of Santeria are brilliantly brought to life in this exciting and critically acclaimed best-seller. If you ever wondered what Santeria is, if you are curious about the rituals and practices of this mysterious religion, and want to delve in its deepest secrets, this book will answer all your questions and much more.

ISBN 0-942272-04-8 5½"x 8½" $16.95

$9.95

The Magic Candle
Facts and Fundamentals of
Candle Burning
By Charmaine Dey

This book contains the fundamentals of ritual candle burning and gives a complete description of:

Types of candles
Color Symbolism
Dressing and Lighting
Oils, Incenses, Seals & Parchments
Planning & Timing

The main object of this book is to help you understand what you are doing, and to create and develop your own techniques and rituals which will surely bring you the results you desire.

ISBN 0-942272-00-5   5½"x 8½

www.OCCULT1.com   Toll Free: 1 (888) OCCULT - 1

Item #003
$14.95

RITUALS AND SPELLS OF SANTERIA

Migene Gonzalez Wippler

Santeria is an earth religion. That is, it is a magico-religious system that has its roots in nature and natural forces. Each orisha or saint is identified with a force of nature and with a human interest or endeavor. Chango, for instance, is the god of fire, thunder and lightning, but he is also the symbol of justice and protects his followers against enemies. He also symbolizes passion and virility and is often invoked in works of seduction. Oshun, on the other hand, symbolizes river waters, love and marriage. She is essentially the archetype of joy and pleasure. Yemaya is identified with the seven seas, but is also the symbol of Motherhood and protects women in their endeavors. Eleggua symbolizes the crossroads, and is the orisha of change and destiny, the one who makes things possible or impossible. He symbolizes the balance of things. Obatala is the father, the symbol of peace and purity. Oya symbolizes the winds and is the owner of the cemetery, the watcher of the doorway between life and death. She is not death, but the awareness of its existence. Oggun is the patron of all metals, and protects farmers, carpenters, butchers, surgeons, mechanics, and all who work with or near metals. He also rules over accidents, which he often causes.

ISBN 0-942272-07-2 5½"x 8½" 134 pages $14.95

TOLL FREE: 1 (888) OCCULT - 1   **WWW.OCCULT1.COM**

ORIGINAL PUBLICATIONS / WWW.OCCULT1.COM / TEL: 888-622-8581

- ☐ The Book on Palo - $21.95
- ☐ Powers of the Orishas - $14.95
- ☐ Santeria; African Magic in Latin America - $16.95
- ☐ Complete Book of Voodoo - $19.95
- ☐ Voodoo & Hoodoo - $16.95
- ☐ Magical Herbal Baths of Santeria - $9.95
- ☐ Rituals & Spells of Santeria - $14.95
- ☐ Shango Santeria & the Orisha of Thunder - $8.95
- ☐ Eshu Ellegua Santeria & the Orisha of the Crossroads - $8.95
- ☐ Yemaya Santeria & the Orisha of the 7 Seas - $8.95
- ☐ Ogun Santeria & the Warrior Orisha of Iron - $8.95
- ☐ Babalu Aye Santeria & the Lord of Pestilence - $8.95
- ☐ Oya Santeria & the Orisha of Storms - $8.95
- ☐ Osanyin Santeria & the Orisha of Plants - $8.95
- ☐ Orunla Santeria & the Orisha of Divination - $8.95
- ☐ Obatala Santeria & the White Robed King of the Orisha - $8.95
- ☐ Ogun Ifa & the Spirit of Iron - $8.95
- ☐ Oshun Ifa & the Spirit of the River - $8.95
- ☐ Ochosi Ifa & the Spirit of the Tracker - $8.95
- ☐ Esu Elegua Ifa & the Divine Messenger - $8.95
- ☐ Obatala Ifa & the Orisha of the White Robe - $8.95
- ☐ Oya Ifa & the Spirit of the Wind - $8.95
- ☐ Yemoja Ifa & the Spirit of the Ocean - $8.95
- ☐ Shango Ifa & the Spirit of Lighting - $8.95
- ☐ Helping Yourself with Selected Prayers Volume 1 - $10.95
- ☐ Helping Yourself with Selected Prayers Volume 2 - $12.95
- ☐ Secrets of the Psalms - $12.95
- ☐ Psalm Workbook - $14.95
- ☐ Psalm Magic - $16.95
- ☐ Success & Power Through Psalms - $9.95
- ☐ Magical Seals Signs & Signatures - $10.95
- ☐ Magical Rituals for Love - $9.95
- ☐ Magical Rituals for Money - $9.95
- ☐ Magical Rituals for Protection - $9.95
- ☐ Unhexing & Jinx Removing - $8.95
- ☐ Complete Book of Baths - $12.95
- ☐ Papa Jim Herbal Magic Workbook - $12.95
- ☐ Papa Jim Magical Oils - $12.95
- ☐ Spiritual Cleansing - $12.95
- ☐ The Magic Candle - $9.95
- ☐ Master Book of Candle Burning - $12.95
- ☐ Gypsy Witch Magic & Spells - $10.95
- ☐ Success Dream Book - $10.95
- ☐ Lucky Star Dream Book - $10.95
- ☐ Lottery Number Dreambook - $14.95
- ☐ 6 & 7 Books of Moses - $16.95
- ☐ 8.9.10 Books of Moses - $12.95

NAME: _____ TELEPHONE: _____

ADDRESS: _____

CITY: _____ STATE: _____ ZIP: _____

ADD SHIPPING FEES: $5.00 FOR THE FIRST BOOK PLUS $1.00 FOR EACH ADDITIONAL BOOK
SEND ORDERS TO: ORIGINALPUBLICATIONS, P.O. BOX 236, OLD BETHPAGE, NY 11804-0236